Name: _____

Address: _____

City/State/Zip: _____

Phone: _____

Email: _____

Class Schedule/Website/Email _____

Class 1 _____

Class 2 _____

Class 3 _____

Class 4 _____

Class 5 _____

Class 6 _____

Class 7 _____

Class 8 _____

Design by April Chloe Terrazas | © 2016 Crazy Brainz, LLC | www.BurntOrangePlanner.com
ISBN#: 978-1-941775-36-3

	SCHEDULE FOR THE YEAR
7a	
8a	
9a	
10a	
11a	
12p	
1p	
2p	
3p	
4p	
5p	

Notes:

Time	SCHEDULE FOR THE YEAR
Morning	
Lunch	
Afternoon	

January	February	March	April	May	June
1	1	1	1	1	1
2	2	2	2	2	2
3	3	3	3	3	3
4	4	4	4	4	4
5	5	5	5	5	5
6	6	6	6	6	6
7	7	7	7	7	7
8	8	8	8	8	8
9	9	9	9	9	9
10	10	10	10	10	10
11	11	11	11	11	11
12	12	12	12	12	12
13	13	13	13	13	13
14	14	14	14	14	14
15	15	15	15	15	15
16	16	16	16	16	16
17	17	17	17	17	17
18	18	18	18	18	18
19	19	19	19	19	19
20	20	20	20	20	20
21	21	21	21	21	21
22	22	22	22	22	22
23	23	23	23	23	23
24	24	24	24	24	24
25	25	25	25	25	25
26	26	26	26	26	26
27	27	27	27	27	27
28	28	28	28	28	28
29	29	29	29	29	29
30		30	30	30	30
31		31		31	

July	August	September	October	November	December
1_____	1_____	1_____	1_____	1_____	1_____
2_____	2_____	2_____	2_____	2_____	2_____
3_____	3_____	3_____	3_____	3_____	3_____
4_____	4_____	4_____	4_____	4_____	4_____
5_____	5_____	5_____	5_____	5_____	5_____
6_____	6_____	6_____	6_____	6_____	6_____
7_____	7_____	7_____	7_____	7_____	7_____
8_____	8_____	8_____	8_____	8_____	8_____
9_____	9_____	9_____	9_____	9_____	9_____
10_____	10_____	10_____	10_____	10_____	10_____
11_____	11_____	11_____	11_____	11_____	11_____
12_____	12_____	12_____	12_____	12_____	12_____
13_____	13_____	13_____	13_____	13_____	13_____
14_____	14_____	14_____	14_____	14_____	14_____
15_____	15_____	15_____	15_____	15_____	15_____
16_____	16_____	16_____	16_____	16_____	16_____
17_____	17_____	17_____	17_____	17_____	17_____
18_____	18_____	18_____	18_____	18_____	18_____
19_____	19_____	19_____	19_____	19_____	19_____
20_____	20_____	20_____	20_____	20_____	20_____
21_____	21_____	21_____	21_____	21_____	21_____
22_____	22_____	22_____	22_____	22_____	22_____
23_____	23_____	23_____	23_____	23_____	23_____
24_____	24_____	24_____	24_____	24_____	24_____
25_____	25_____	25_____	25_____	25_____	25_____
26_____	26_____	26_____	26_____	26_____	26_____
27_____	27_____	27_____	27_____	27_____	27_____
28_____	28_____	28_____	28_____	28_____	28_____
29_____	29_____	29_____	29_____	29_____	29_____
30_____	30_____	30_____	30_____	30_____	30_____
31_____	31_____		31_____		31_____

July	August	September
October	November	December

January	February	March
April	May	June

Name	Email	Phone #

Name	Email	Phone #
Name	Email	Phone #

Professor Name	Website

MONTH:_____

Monday	Tuesday	Wednesday

Monday	Tuesday	Wednesday

MONTH:_____

Thursday	Friday	Saturday/Sunday

MONTH:_____

Monday	Tuesday	Wednesday
Monday	Tuesday	Wednesday

MONTH:_____

Thursday	Friday	Saturday/Sunday

Thursday	Friday	Saturday/Sunday

MONTH:_____

Monday	Tuesday	Wednesday

Monday	Tuesday	Wednesday

MONTH:_____

Thursday	Friday	Saturday/Sunday

MONTH:_____

Monday	Tuesday	Wednesday

Monday	Tuesday	Wednesday

MONTH:_____

Thursday	Friday	Saturday/Sunday

MONTH:_____

Monday	Tuesday	Wednesday

Monday	Tuesday	Wednesday

MONTH:_____

Thursday	Friday	Saturday/Sunday

MONTH:_____

Monday	Tuesday	Wednesday

Monday	Tuesday	Wednesday

MONTH:_____

Thursday	Friday	Saturday/Sunday

MONTH:_____

Monday	Tuesday	Wednesday

Monday	Tuesday	Wednesday

MONTH:_____

Thursday	Friday	Saturday/Sunday

Thursday	Friday	Saturday/Sunday

MONTH:_____

Monday	Tuesday	Wednesday

Monday	Tuesday	Wednesday

MONTH:_____

Thursday	Friday	Saturday/Sunday

Thursday	Friday	Saturday/Sunday

MONTH:_____

Monday	Tuesday	Wednesday

Monday	Tuesday	Wednesday

MONTH:_____

Thursday	Friday	Saturday/Sunday

Thursday	Friday	Saturday/Sunday

MONTH:_____

Monday	Tuesday	Wednesday

Monday	Tuesday	Wednesday

MONTH:_____

Thursday	Friday	Saturday/Sunday

Thursday	Friday	Saturday/Sunday

MONTH:_____

Monday	Tuesday	Wednesday

| Monday | Tuesday | Wednesday |

MONTH:_____

Thursday	Friday	Saturday/Sunday

Thursday	Friday	Saturday/Sunday

MONTH:_____

Monday	Tuesday	Wednesday

Monday	Tuesday	Wednesday

MONTH:_____

Thursday	Friday	Saturday/Sunday

Thursday	Friday	Saturday/Sunday

Important This Week

Goals

To Do

Week/Month: Student Planner

Day	Schedule	Homework	HW done
M			
T			
W			
Th			
F			

Sat/Sun	Projects/Tests

Important This Week

Goals

To Do

Day	Schedule	Homework	HW done
M			
T			
W			
Th			
F			

Sat/Sun	Projects/Tests

Important This Week

Goals

To Do

Week/Month:

Day	Schedule	Homework	HW done
M			
T			
W			
Th			
F			

Sat/Sun	Projects/Tests

Important This Week

Goals

To Do

Day	Schedule	Homework	HW done
M			
T			
W			
Th			
F			

Sat/Sun	Projects/Tests

Important This Week

Goals

To Do

Day	Schedule	Homework	HW done
M			
T			
W			
Th			
F			

Sat/Sun	**Projects/Tests**

Important This Week

Goals

To Do

Day	Schedule	Homework	HW done
M			
T			
W			
Th			
F			

Sat/Sun	Projects/Tests

Important This Week

Goals

To Do

Week/Month: Student Planner

Day	Schedule	Homework	HW done
M			
T			
W			
Th			
F			

Sat/Sun

Projects/Tests

Important This Week

Goals

To Do

Day	Schedule	Homework	HW done
M			
T			
W			
Th			
F			

Sat/Sun	**Projects/Tests**

Important This Week

Goals

To Do

Week/Month: Student Planner

Day	Schedule	Homework	HW done
M			
T			
W			
Th			
F			

Sat/Sun	Projects/Tests

Important This Week

Goals

To Do

Day	Schedule	Homework	HW done
M			
T			
W			
Th			
F			

Sat/Sun	**Projects/Tests**

Important This Week

Goals

To Do

Day	Schedule	Homework	HW done
M			
T			
W			
Th			
F			

Sat/Sun	Projects/Tests

Important This Week

Goals

To Do

Important This Week

Day	Schedule	Homework	HW done
M			
T			
W			
Th			
F			

Sat/Sun	**Projects/Tests**

Important This Week

Goals

To Do

Week/Month:

Day	Schedule	Homework	HW done
M			
T			
W			
Th			
F			

Sat/Sun	Projects/Tests

Important This Week

Goals

To Do

Week/Month: Student Planner

Day	Schedule	Homework	HW done
M			
T			
W			
Th			
F			

Sat/Sun	**Projects/Tests**

Important This Week

Goals

To Do

Week/Month: Student Planner

Day	Schedule	Homework	HW done
M			
T			
W			
Th			
F			

Sat/Sun	Projects/Tests

Important This Week

Goals

To Do

Important This Week

Week/Month: Student Planner

Day	Schedule	Homework	HW done
M			
T			
W			
Th			
F			

Sat/Sun	**Projects/Tests**

Important This Week

Goals

To Do

Day	Schedule	Homework	HW done
M			
T			
W			
Th			
F			

Sat/Sun	Projects/Tests

Important This Week

Goals

To Do

Day	Schedule	Homework	HW done
M			
T			
W			
Th			
F			

Sat/Sun	Projects/Tests

Important This Week

Goals

To Do

Day	Schedule	Homework	HW done
M			
T			
W			
Th			
F			

Sat/Sun	Projects/Tests

Important This Week

Goals

To Do

Day	Schedule	Homework	HW done
M			
T			
W			
Th			
F			

Sat/Sun		**Projects/Tests**

Important This Week

Goals

To Do

Important This Week

Week/Month:

Student Planner

Day	Schedule	Homework	HW done
M			
T			
W			
Th			
F			

Sat/Sun		Projects/Tests

Important This Week

Goals

To Do

Day	Schedule	Homework	HW done
M			
T			
W			
Th			
F			

Sat/Sun	Projects/Tests

Important This Week

Goals

To Do

Week/Month:

Student Planner

Day	Schedule	Homework	HW done
M			
T			
W			
Th			
F			

Sat/Sun	Projects/Tests

Important This Week

Goals

To Do

Day	Schedule	Homework	HW done
M			
T			
W			
Th			
F			

Sat/Sun

Projects/Tests

Important This Week

Goals

To Do

Day	Schedule	Homework	HW done
M			
T			
W			
Th			
F			

Sat/Sun	Projects/Tests

Important This Week

Goals

To Do

Day	Schedule	Homework	HW done
M			
T			
W			
Th			
F			

Sat/Sun	Projects/Tests

Important This Week

Goals

To Do

Day	Schedule	Homework	HW done
M			
T			
W			
Th			
F			

Sat/Sun	Projects/Tests

Important This Week

Goals

To Do

Day	Schedule	Homework	HW done
M			
T			
W			
Th			
F			

Sat/Sun	Projects/Tests

Important This Week

Goals

To Do

Week/Month:

Day	Schedule	Homework	HW done
M			
T			
W			
Th			
F			

Sat/Sun	Projects/Tests

Important This Week

Goals

To Do

Day	Schedule	Homework	HW done
M			
T			
W			
Th			
F			

Sat/Sun	Projects/Tests

Important This Week

Goals

To Do

Day	Schedule	Homework	HW done
M			
T			
W			
Th			
F			

Sat/Sun	Projects/Tests

Important This Week

Goals

To Do

Day	Schedule	Homework	HW done
M			
T			
W			
Th			
F			

Sat/Sun	Projects/Tests

Important This Week

Goals

To Do

Week/Month: _____

Student Planner

Day	Schedule	Homework	HW done
M			
T			
W			
Th			
F			

Sat/Sun	Projects/Tests

Important This Week

Goals

To Do

Day	Schedule	Homework	HW done
M			
T			
W			
Th			
F			

Sat/Sun	Projects/Tests

Important This Week

Goals

To Do

Important This Week

Week/Month:

Day	Schedule	Homework	HW done
M			
T			
W			
Th			
F			

Sat/Sun	**Projects/Tests**

Important This Week

Goals

To Do

Week/Month:

Student Planner

Day	Schedule	Homework	HW done
M			
T			
W			
Th			
F			

Sat/Sun	Projects/Tests

Important This Week

Goals

To Do

Week/Month: Student Planner

Day	Schedule	Homework	HW done
M			
T			
W			
Th			
F			

Sat/Sun		Projects/Tests

Important This Week

Goals

To Do

Week/Month:

Student Planner

Day	Schedule	Homework	HW done
M			
T			
W			
Th			
F			

Sat/Sun	Projects/Tests

Important This Week

Goals

To Do

Week/Month:

Day	Schedule	Homework	HW done
M			
T			
W			
Th			
F			

Sat/Sun	Projects/Tests
Day	

Important This Week

Goals

To Do

Day	Schedule	Homework	HW done
M			
T			
W			
Th			
F			

Sat/Sun	Projects/Tests
M	

Important This Week

Goals

To Do

Week/Month: Student Planner

Day	Schedule	Homework	HW done
M			
T			
W			
Th			
F			

Sat/Sun | | **Projects/Tests**

Important This Week

Goals

To Do

Day	Schedule	Homework	HW done
M			
T			
W			
Th			
F			

Sat/Sun	Projects/Tests

Important This Week

Goals

To Do

Day	Schedule	Homework	HW done
M			
T			
W			
Th			
F			

Sat/Sun	Projects/Tests
Day	

Important This Week

Goals

To Do

Week/Month:

Day	Schedule	Homework	HW done
M			
T			
W			
Th			
F			

Sat/Sun

Projects/Tests

Important This Week

Goals

To Do

Day	Schedule	Homework	HW done
M			
T			
W			
Th			
F			

Sat/Sun	Projects/Tests

Important This Week

Goals

To Do

Day	Schedule	Homework	HW done
M			
T			
W			
Th			
F			

Sat/Sun		**Projects/Tests**
Day		

Important This Week

Goals

To Do

Day	Schedule	Homework	HW done
M			
T			
W			
Th			
F			

Sat/Sun	Projects/Tests

Important This Week

Goals

To Do

Week/Month: Student Planner

Day	Schedule	Homework	HW done
M			
T			
W			
Th			
F			

Sat/Sun	Projects/Tests

Important This Week

Goals

To Do

Day	Schedule	Homework	HW done
M			
T			
W			
Th			
F			

Sat/Sun	Projects/Tests

Important This Week

Goals

To Do

Important This Week

Day	Schedule	Homework	HW done
M			
T			
W			
Th			
F			

Sat/Sun	Projects/Tests

Important This Week

Goals

To Do

Day	Schedule	Homework	HW done
M			
T			
W			
Th			
F			

Sat/Sun	Projects/Tests

Important This Week

Goals

To Do

Day	Schedule	Homework	HW done
M			
T			
W			
Th			
F			

Sat/Sun	Projects/Tests

Important This Week

Goals

To Do

Week/Month: _____

Day	Schedule	Homework	HW done
M			
T			
W			
Th			
F			

Sat/Sun

Projects/Tests

Important This Week

Goals

To Do

Important This Week

Week/Month: Student Planner

Day	Schedule	Homework	HW done
M			
T			
W			
Th			
F			

Sat/Sun	Projects/Tests

Important This Week

Goals

To Do

Week/Month: _____

Student Planner

Day	Schedule	Homework	HW done
M			
T			
W			
Th			
F			

Sat/Sun		Projects/Tests
M		

www.ingramcontent.com/pod-product-compliance
Lightning Source LLC
LaVergne TN
LVHW070841080426

835513LV00024B/2423